PILOTS
FLY PLANES

▲ ● ▲ ● ▼ ● ▲ ● ▼ ● ▲ ● ▼ ● ▲ ▲ ● ▼ ● ▲ ● ▲ ● ▼ ● ▲ ● ▲ ●

Design and electronic page composition
Lindaanne Donohoe Design

Photo research
Feldman & Associates, Inc.

● ▲ ● ▼ ● ▲ ● ● ▲ ● ▼ ● ▲ ●

Picture Acknowledgments

©**William B. Folsum**—5, 13

David R. Frazier Photolibrary—©David Frazier, 20

©**Patrickcone Photography**—9

PhotoEdit—10, ©Tom McCarthy, 7; ©John Neubauer, 15; ©Vic Bider, 30

©**SuperStock International, Inc.**—3, 4, 11, 12, 14, 17, 18, 26

Unicorn Stock Photos—©Jean Higgins, cover, 19,22, 23, 27, 28;
©Aneal Vohra, 6; ©Tom McCarthy, 8; ©Denny Bailly, 16;
©Steve Bourgeois, 21, 24; ©Travis Evans, 25

● ▲ ● ▼ ● ▲ ● ● ▲ ● ▼ ● ▲ ●

Library of Congress Cataloging-in-Publication Data

Robinson, Fay.

Pilots fly planes/Fay Robinson.
p.   cm.
Includes index.
Summary: Explains the work of a pilot by taking the
reader step-by-step through a typical day.
ISBN 1-56766-308-7 (hardcover)
1. Aeronautics — Vocational guidance — Juvenile literature.
2. Airplanes — Piloting — Vocational guidance — Juvenile literature.
[1. Aeronautics — Vocational guidance. 2. Air pilots. 3. Airplanes — Piloting.]
I. Title.

TL561.R63   1996   96-7199
629.132'52'023—dc20   CIP
                                                            AC

▲ ▲

PILOTS
FLY PLANES

By Fay Robinson

THE CHILD'S WORLD®

Up, up, up!
Higher and higher and higher!
An airplane soars into the sky.

ZOOOM! ZOOM!

Where is it going?

How does it get there?

Nearly a hundred people
helped this plane get ready to fly.
Now the pilot is in charge.

Today, this pilot was at the airport
at six o'clock in the morning.
It was still dark outside.

First, she reads all about her flight. There
is a lot to know! She goes into her plane
before any of the passengers get on board.

This plane is called a 727.
It holds 147 people. It can fly up
to 2,400 miles without stopping.

All pilots and co-pilots wear headsets.
They must hear directions from
the flight tower.

They check and set each button, knob, and dial. Every single one is important. They check the outside of the plane too.

Everything is okay.

The passengers get on board.

The engines start and the plane starts
to rumble. *RRRM!*   *RRRM!*   *RRRM!*

As it rushes down the runway,
the plane picks up speed.
VROOM! VROOM! VROOM!

When it reaches about 150 miles
per hour, the plane lifts into the air.
ZOOM!

The sky is cloudy. Suddenly, the plane breaks
through the clouds into the sunny sky.

The pilot turns the plane onto
its course.

How does the pilot know where to go?
He or she follows a map. The plane's
computers give the pilot information, too.

And the pilot gets help
from people on the ground called
air-traffic controllers.

Sometimes a plane hits windy spots
in the sky. *THUMP! THUMP!*
The plane bounces up and down.

The pilot tells the passengers not
to worry. He steers the plane away
from the bumpy air.

Soon, it's time to land. The pilot talks to
air-traffic controllers at the airport ahead.

They tell him which runway to land on.
The pilot turns down the engines.

WHIIINE! The plane slows down.
It heads back through the clouds.

Up ahead, the pilot can see the city.

He can see the runway.

Touchdown!
The pilot puts on the brakes.
SCHREEEECH! SCHREEEECH!

The pilot shuts down all
the systems and says
good-bye to the passengers.

Time to go home?
Not when you're a pilot!

This pilot hurries through the airport
for her next flight.

She boards her next plane.
And everything starts again.

Questions and Answers

What is a pilot's day like?

Airline pilots fly up to four flights in a day. Most of the time, they don't fly home at the end of a work day. Instead, they spend the night in a hotel. The next day they might fly another three or four flights, and stay in another hotel. Finally, after three or four days, pilots fly home. They rest a few days before they fly again.

Why do pilots wear uniforms?

Pilots wear uniforms so that people can recognize them. The pilot is in charge of everything that happens on a plane, so it's important that everyone knows who he or she is.

How can you become a pilot?

Pilots must go to flight school for several years. There, they learn about weather, computers, and how to operate a plane. Then they must pass a test to be allowed to fly. Every year, they must take the test again.

What kind of people make good pilots?

Flying a large plane is a very important job. The safety of hundreds of people is in the pilot's hands. So pilots are healthy and strong. They are calm people who can take care of problems without getting upset. And because they work with so many people, they are friendly and outgoing.

What kinds of airplanes do pilots fly?

The 727 is just one kind of plane. There are small planes that carry only a couple of passengers. And there are much larger planes that carry up to 400 passengers. There are planes that carry only mail and packages. There are even planes that carry cars and trucks. Every kind of plane is different, and pilots must get special training for each kind of plane that they fly.

Glossary

airplane—a machine with wings that uses the power of its engines to fly through the air

airport—the place built for airplanes

air-traffic controllers—people who are in charge of keeping track of all the planes in the air. They tell the pilots what part of the sky is open. They make sure that all planes fly in the space that belongs to them.

computers—special machines that can hold information and can quickly give answers

co-pilot—person that helps the pilot fly the plane

course—the place or path that something takes

engines—a machine built with many different parts that is used to give power objects, such as cars, planes, trains, and other machines

flight tower—tall building at airports that holds the people and the special machines needed to help pilots take off and land safely

headsets—a special radio that carries sound from the pilot and co-pilot to people on the ground

map—the picture of the land that shows rivers, mountains, cities, and other landmarks for travellers

passengers—people who pay money to travel on planes, buses, or trains

pilot—the person in charge of flying the plane and keeping passengers safe

runway—long stretches of concrete built for take offs and landings

systems—the complete set of instruments, knobs, dials, buttons, that are put together in order to run a machines, such as an airplane

FAY ROBINSON is an early childhood specialist who lives and works in the Chicago area. She received a bachelor's degree in Child Study from Tufts University and a master's degree in Education from Northwestern University. She has taught preschool and elementary children and is the author of several picture books.